Free Indeed

A Roadmap to Victorious Living

By Ronda S Barnes

Free Indeed
A Road Map to Victorious Living

Dedication

This book is dedicated to those Christians that are growing in their walk with Christ. If you receive nothing else from this book, know that God loves you and Jesus is sitting at the right hand of the father making intercession just for you. Trust God as you go from glory to glory and faith to faith.

Stop Stressing and Breathe-
It's not that deep!

Contents

Introduction — 1

Doing It Afraid — 4

Grace And Peace Be Multiplied — 11

What You Feed Will Lead — 17

Condemnation: Such A Lie Of The Enemy — 23

Lead Us Not Into Temptation — 28

About The Author — 34

Introduction

The Christian walk is one that ebbs and flows. At times, you may find yourself on the mountaintop, and at other times in the valley. Yet, your decision to give God a "yes" is one of the most important decisions of your life! When I sat down to write this book, my initial intent was to write a simple devotional to help believers meditate on and grow in the Word, but the Lord had other plans. While reflecting on my journey, I realized my walk has not followed the "typical" path often portrayed for most believers.

In so many situations, I have seen God move in my life in ways that most people said He would not move. I can remember feeling so much like a failure in the beginning because I loved God so much, but just could not get this walk right. There was always this knowing inside of me that I was called for more, but the way I had learned the Christian walk, whether by what was seen or taught, was challenging. It felt impossible to achieve. I struggled in so many areas that I was either too afraid to talk to anyone about it, or when I did, their advice was not applicable to my situation. I simply could not walk it out. Many of my perspectives and experiences did not align with the narrative being portrayed, and deep down, I began to believe that I must be a heathen destined for hell because I could not live the way they were telling me to live.

That is when I truly started seeking the Lord for direction. My heart was genuinely pure toward Him, and although I struggled with different areas of sin, I refused to believe that I could not succeed in this walk of faith. The more I opened up and became transparent before the Lord, the more He began to provide me with strategies and guidance to overcome some incredibly difficult situations. As I wrote, it became clear that if I felt this way, I knew others must feel the same. From that realization, **Free Indeed: A Roadmap to Victorious Living** was born.

This book is one of my most vulnerable works. I openly share intimate parts of my life with the hope that you, the reader, will find freedom and breakthrough in your own journey. If I can help shift your mindset and show you that you're not a lost cause, that's more than enough for me! LOL! The power of God is so much greater than you know! As you read this book, I encourage you to let God speak to your heart and strengthen you on your journey!

Dear God,

I come before You now on behalf of the one reading this book. Thank You for leading them to this place of safety in You where they can openly bare their soul without guilt, shame, or fear. You know the deepest parts of our heart and every choice we've made along our journey- good, bad, and everything in between- yet You're still deeply in love with us.

My prayer is that the eyes of their understanding are enlightened to Your hope, love, and heart for them. Strengthen their faith, cover their thoughts, empower, inspire, and refuel them on their journey with You. I speak now to every area of shame, guilt, condemnation, and fear, and I bind you from operating in their lives. I release the breaker anointing to break every yoke of bondage, and I release the yoke of the Lord that makes every yoke easy and every burden light. As they learn, open their ears to hear. Unblock every clogged area and allow them to hear clearly with the ears of God. I break the fog of confusion that seeks to distort the words on this page, and I release the spirit of truth to illuminate every dark place. Cause their soul to be made whole and align their lives with Your will.

Destiny come forth in Jesus' name! Purpose be defined NOW in Jesus' name! Vision be made clear now in Jesus Name! Healing manifest in the name of Jesus! Thank You, Lord, for Your faithfulness in drawing towards us daily and for Your concern over the things that concern us.

Forever growing in victory,

Amen!

Chapter 1
Doing It Afraid

There is no fear in love, but perfect love drives out fear, because fear involves punishment. The one who fears has not been perfected in love.
John 4:18 (ESV)

Fear is such a common emotion these days. From anxiety and phobias to fear of man, the language of fear has become so familiar that people have begun to wear it as a badge of honor. In the way I was raised, embracing, or accepting fear was never an option. I can remember being very young and struggling with nightmares. At times, I would be so afraid that I could not even get out of my bed. When I could finally muster up the courage to run to my parents' room, my mom would wake up and take me back to my room. Once there, we would sit, pray, and she would give me scriptures relating to fear and what God says about it.

She would not allow me to sleep in her and my father's bed nor would she stay down there in my room until I fell asleep. She gave me the tools to overcome, and she gave me the space to learn how to use them. The very first scripture I remember memorizing around the age of five was 2 Timothy 1:7, "For God hath not given us the spirit of fear; but, of power, and of love, and of a sound mind." I remember feeling afraid, reciting this scripture, and meditating on it in my mind until I could finally fall asleep again. As I grew older, the fear surrounding my dreams became so overwhelming that there were times I had to sleep with the lights on in my room.

At one point, it seemed like the more I prayed, the more intense the fear became. The only thing that released the fear was to declare, "The Blood of Jesus!" Even into my mid-twenties, I struggled with this kind of fear, despite knowing God! Though I had a relationship with Him, for some reason, this paralyzing fear would strike me around the same time every night. It was not until I grew tired of being afraid that I decided to confront it. By then, I had started noticing a pattern- the enemy would attack me in my sleep between 11:55 p.m. and 12:05 a.m. every time.

One particular night, I could feel the fear creeping in as I drifted off to sleep, but I was so sleepy that I couldn't fight it. When the attack came, I managed to wake myself up. I sat straight up in bed, trembling and sweating, with my heart pounding so loudly that I could hear it in my ears. I said, "God, I am not dealing with this anymore! Why is this happening and what do I need to do at this moment?" With my voice quivering and my body shaking with fear, I began to pray and worship God. Yet, the more I prayed, the more intense the fear seemed to grow. But I pressed in harder, worshiping and praising God for His goodness and mercy. Then it happened. The presence of the Lord filled the room, and I began to weep. As His sweet presence surrounded me, peace flooded my entire body, and a deep calm settled in my spirit. I drifted off to sleep, resting in the arms of the Lord.

Through that experience the Lord began to teach me about my authority, who He is, and the tools he released to us to help us walk out this life with power, authority, and boldness. Romans 8:14-17 (ESV) says,

> "For all who are led by the Spirit of God are sons of God. For you did not receive the spirit of slavery to fall back into fear, but you have received the Spirit of adoption as sons, by whom we cry, "Abba! Father!" The Spirit himself bears witness with

our spirit that we are children of God, and if children, then heirs—heirs of God and fellow heirs with Christ, provided we suffer with him in order that we may also be glorified with him."

These scriptures let us know who we are and the position we have in the Kingdom of God. Not only are we sons of God, but we are also joint heirs with Jesus. Merriam Webster's dictionary defines **heir** as *one who inherits or is entitled to succeed to a hereditary rank, title, or office; one who receives or is entitled to receive something other than property from a parent or predecessor.* As joint heirs with Jesus, we are entitled to succeed to a hereditary rank, title, or office because GOD is our father through the work of the Cross. Ephesians 2:4-6 (ESV) declares,

"But God, being rich in mercy, because of the great love with which he loved us, even when we were dead in our trespasses, made us alive together with Christ—by grace you have been saved— and raised us up with him and seated us with him in the heavenly places in Christ Jesus,"

Our position in Christ is one that is seated in heavenly places in Christ Jesus. This means in Christ, we have a full-grown Jesus inside of us! Luke 10:19 (ESV) says,

"Behold, I have given you authority to tread on serpents and scorpions, and over all the power of the enemy, and nothing shall hurt you."

We have authority over all the power of the enemy, and nothing shall by any means hurt us. Hallelujah! What a promise from the Lord!! As believers, it is vital for us to meditate on Scripture and let the Word take root in our hearts. The Word of God is one of our most powerful weapons as we overcome areas of fear in our lives. Heb 4:12 (ESV) declares,

> "For the word of God is living and active, sharper than any two-edged sword, piercing to the division of soul and of spirit, of joints and of marrow, and discerning the thoughts and intentions of the heart."

The Word of God discerns the thoughts and intentions of the heart. As the years went by, I would try to escape the fear that came over me at night, hoping it would eventually fade away. That was not the case. I had to do my part by putting the Word in action to see it begin to manifest in my life. This would not have happened if I continued to run away from the spirit of fear that showed up every night. I had to face my fear.

So often we wait until we no longer feel the fear before we step out. Fear is one of the main tactics the enemy uses to keep you from fulfilling the purpose that God has for your life. Battling the spirit of fear in my sleep was directly linked correlated to my call to the ministry of deliverance. The enemy tried to use that tactic from the moment of my birth to instill fear and prevent me from tearing down the kingdom of darkness. How can you fight the enemy if you have a deep-rooted foundation of fear where he's concerned? You can't!

At just five years old, my mom began to lay the foundation for me, providing the weapons I needed to fight the spirit of fear. Those same weapons carried me and established a key mindset that sticks with me today. Fear is not an option! When fear tries to come against me, I intentionally choose to stand in the face of fear and say "NO! I WILL NOT BE AFRAID!" We must know who we are and the authority we have as joint heirs with Jesus and begin to resist the tactics of the enemy.

Oftentimes, when we struggle with fear, it means that there is an area in our heart that does not know the perfect love of God as our Father. Wherever fear arises, we lack revelation of His perfect love in that area. For example, if you struggle with confidence, it is connected to your internal perception of yourself. John 4:17-18 (ESV) explains,

> "By this is love perfected with us, so that we may have confidence for the day of judgment, because as he is so also are we in this world. There is no fear in love, but perfect love casts out fear. For fear has to do with punishment, and whoever fears has not been perfected in love."

According to this scripture, when love is perfected, it releases confidence. This confidence is not in our own ability, but in the ability of the One who created us. Recall that verse 18 says fear involves punishment. That is why the death, burial, and resurrection of Jesus is so life-changing for believers. His death freed us from the penalty and power of sin, allowing us to receive His love, perfected in us through the blood of Jesus. Because He knew we could not get it right on our own, God sent His son Jesus, the perfect manifestation of love, as a sacrifice to pay the price for everything we have done, would do, and even could do on the cross. Any sin that could ever be committed has been nailed on the cross with Jesus and died with Him. That is why when we repent, we're placed back in right standing with the Father as if we never sinned. We are not depending on our work or abilities. We are leaning on and walking in His love! When you choose to do it afraid, you have heaven's backing by the blood of Jesus to cover you.

Dear God,

Thank You for the work of the Cross. Through the shed blood of Jesus, we have become joint heirs with Jesus, those who are led by the spirit of God and seated in heavenly places. Because of this, Your Word assures us that we have authority over all the power of the enemy, including fear. At this moment, reveal Your perfect love in the area where fear has tried to keep me complacent, not walking in the purpose and plan You have established for me. Open my mind and my heart to the mind of God to live a bold life in full fellowship with You, know You as my Father, and accept the love You have given to me even before the foundation of the world.

In Jesus' Name,

Amen

Chapter 2
Grace and Peace Be Multiplied

His divine power has given us everything we need for life and godliness through the knowledge of Him who called us by His own glory and excellence.
2 Peter 1:3 (ESV)

As a single mother, I am quite used to making things happen. If the kids need clothes, I make it happen. If the car breaks down, I get what is needed and make it happen. If the grandkids need diapers, I make it happen. I cannot say I have always been like this- my mother and father always took care of my siblings and me throughout my childhood. We never wanted for anything. When I became a mother, the shame of having a child out of wedlock- not once, but three times- led me to create an environment in which I was filled with pride and very resistant to accepting help.

Often, when you are in a difficult place in your life, you barely have enough strength to bear the weight of what you've done or are currently facing. The last thing you need is ridicule, negative words, guilt, and shame from others or yourself. I taught myself to rely on no one and make things happen on my own. Through the tears, brokenness, hurt, and pain, I pushed forward and mastered the art of smiling through it all. But beneath the surface, I was falling apart, and I had no idea how to cope with the weight I was carrying.

I would go to church, participate in praise and worship, pray, and minister to others, but as soon as I left, I turned to smoking cigarettes, engaging in premarital sex, masturbation, and doing whatever else I could to numb the pain and pressure of the internal battle raging inside me. I hated sinning against

God, but when the weight became overwhelming, I would cave because it offered me temporary relief. I just wanted to relieve the pain of unmet expectations, broken promises, and continued rejection I felt in so many areas of my life. As the years went by, God began to show me that my response to hardship was less about the outward actions and more about the condition of my heart.

The pain came because of the needs in my heart that were never met. When the void of these unmet needs overwhelmed me, instead of reaching out for help to the only One that could satisfy, I would reach for the things that I could physically touch and experience. This was a result of a familiar spirit of rebellion in my bloodline that would rear its head in my moments of disappointment. I could not trust that God would help. I was angry that He did not meet the need in the way I felt that He should. I convinced myself that I could deal with the pain and just repent. But that was not God's heart for me.

With each cycle, I would get to a place where I was tired of going back and forth, and I would fast to break the pattern of backsliding. During these times, the Lord showed me Romans 12:1 (ESV),

> "I appeal to you therefore, brothers, by the mercies of God,
> to present your bodies as a living sacrifice, holy and acceptable
> to God, which is your spiritual worship."

I had to realize that if I am to truly profess to believe in Jesus and live according to the Word of God, it means that my life is not my own and neither is my body. Apostle Paul said, "I appeal to you therefore, brothers, by the mercies of God…" When you are in this type of war over your flesh, the mercies of God are necessary. The word **mercy** in this scripture is the Greek word **oiktirmos** meaning *compassion, pity, mercy, bowels in which compassion resides, a* *heart of compassion, emotions, longings, manifestations of pity.* To activate this level of mercy and compassion, you must humble yourself before the Lord and admit that you need help.

This kind of fight within the will attacks the identity of the believer because it contradicts what you know you should desire in your heart. For me, I wanted to love myself, but I did not feel worthy of my Father's love because of the mistakes I had made. There was always this subconscious excuse saying, "It's okay if you fall because God knew you were trying." But that was not really the case.

In this season, I learned that the struggle of the will is overcome by making a decision!

This is when 2 Peter 1:2-4 (ESV) began to come alive for me.

> "May grace and peace be multiplied to you in the knowledge of God and of Jesus our Lord. His divine power has granted to us all things that pertain to life and godliness, through the knowledge of him who called us to his own glory and excellence, by which he has granted to us his precious and very great promises, so that through them you may become partakers of the divine nature, having escaped from the corruption that is in the world because of sinful desire."

This scripture literally became my life's creed through every area of my life, both good and difficult! As I walked out my process to freedom, God began showing me that I did not have to go through this process alone. Even in the areas where I struggled with sin, He never discarded me. He did for me what others said He would not do! Despite my sinful behavior, He created a safe environment for me to come to Him with no reservation. I did not have to stop what I was doing. He never said to me "You can't come to me in any kind of way." Amid my struggles, I would partner with Him, and we worked together to turn things around. In the pain of my desperation to satisfy my unmet needs, I would sit with Him, and together we would read Isaiah 58:11 (ESV).

> "And the Lord will guide you continually and satisfy your desire in scorched places and make your bones strong; and you shall be like a watered garden, like a spring of water, whose waters do not fail."

In this scripture, **scorched places** are also places of **drought** or **dry places.** The enemy uses these cycles of sin (any sin, not just sexual sin) to cause a separation from God and delay in moving forward with the plans of God for our lives. Oftentimes, when we sin against God in any manner our first response is to do as Adam and Eve did in the garden- run and hide ourselves in shame. This shame causes us to avoid intimacy with God. Religion tells us we must "clean ourselves up" before we come before the Lord, but that is simply not true.

On my journey, I learned just how much more His grace and peace were multiplied in those areas of dry places. God provided everything I needed for life and godliness through His power. I did not have to figure it out on my own. He sent people to minister to my heart. In our devotion time, He revealed wounded areas and places of trauma that needed healing, and He broke through the self-protecting rebellion in my heart by His word as I grew in my knowledge of Him.

The more I learned about His character and nature, the more I began to see that He never switches up on me when I would sin. He patiently waits for me to realize He is always there, and when I run back to Him, we pick up even better than where we left off. Through His divine power, I began to see that the time between my sin and my coming back to the Lord became shorter and shorter. Eventually, I was strong enough to resist and the cycle was broken.

Dear God,

Thank You for providing everything we need for life and godliness. You never intended for us to walk this life alone. In Your intentionality, You have provided everything we need before we need it and for that, I am grateful. In this moment, I lift up the one reading this chapter and I ask that You heal every broken area that the enemy would use to cause separation and introduce a spirit of delay in their lives. I break all shame, guilt, and grief off them now by the power of the blood of Jesus and release a spirit of adoption over them. As sons of God, You said we can come to You and You would not turn us away. We know that it is only in You that they can overcome the bondage of the will to truly walk out Your will for their life. Thank You for never leaving us alone in this journey.

In Jesus' Name,

Amen

Chapter 3
What You Feed Will Lead

For as he thinks in his heart, so is he...
Proverbs 23:7 (NKJV)

Years ago, my attitude was unbelievably bad. I was mean, sharp, and very blunt with no regard to how words came out of my mouth. I had a way with words that could build you up and make you feel as though you were on top of the world. However, if you hurt me, I would cut you all the way down and go for the jugular! Before I understood the power of my words and the calling of God on my life, weighing my words was never anything that came to mind.

I can remember a day when I was out for lunch with a close friend. We gave the server our orders and continued talking. When the food arrived, it felt like time stood still. I went to take a bite, noticing my friend watching me closely, as if she was waiting to see how I would react. Then she said, "Is your food okay? Because if it's not, you don't have to say anything. I'll call the waitress." The food was fine, but I was puzzled, so I asked her why she reacted that way. She responded, "I didn't want you to go off."

In that moment, I felt annoyed because she pointed out an area in me that I had not seen as a problem before—but she was right. I began to remember the times my rudeness caused others to avoid me, stay away from me, and sometimes even cry from my response. We finished our lunch, but on the ride home, I began talking to the Lord. My heart desire was to be a good witness and look like Jesus.

When God reveals parts of our character that do not align with His character, it can be difficult, but necessary to receive so we can see His transformative power at work in our lives. Luke 6:45 (ESV) says,

> "A good person produces good things from the treasury of a good heart, and an evil person produces evil things from the treasury of an evil heart. What you say flows from what is in your heart."

The word **good** in this scripture means *pleasant, agreeable, joyful, happy, excellent, distinguished, upright, and honorable.* The word **evil** means *hurtful, calamitous, vicious, mischief, malice, guilt, grievous, harm, malicious, wicked, annoyances, bad, of a bad nature or condition.*

Oftentimes, when we hear **evil**, we reject it because it is believed that generally we're all good people. However, this is not always the case. When I reflected on my actions towards people, even though my intent was not to be evil, the abundance of my heart showed an area of evilness, and I had to accept that. If we ever want to break negative cycles, we must first see it, accept it, and then allow the Holy Spirit to begin dealing with that area.

When I initially began doing the work, it was so hard. The Lord began to show me the areas of woundedness in my heart that caused my responses. In this case, when I felt as though someone was trying to "get over" on me or "keep me from something that I deserved," a trigger was hit and I automatically lashed out. I could recognize the trigger but could not stop my response. Once things calmed down, I felt dirty, grieved, embarrassed, and ashamed. My life felt like an emotional yo-yo, constantly jerking up and down, and I did not know how to make it stop. As I prayed for guidance, God began to talk to me about fasting according to Isaiah 58:6 (KJV).

> "Is not this the fast that I have chosen? to loose the bands of wickedness, to undo the heavy burdens, and to let the oppressed go free, and that ye break every yoke?"

Our flesh or our carnal nature has an appetite. This natural nature has proclivities and wiring that, when left of its own accord, will run rampant. My flesh had become accustomed to being temporarily satisfied by the evil responses of my heart. Through the reading of the Word and by the power of the Holy Spirit, I was able to recognize this as being the opposite of His nature. Nevertheless, this was not a quick change. These responses had been a natural part of my actions for so long that they had become a weight of oppression and a yoke of bondage.

Isaiah 56:6 talks about the fast that was chosen to loose the bands of wickedness…and to let the oppressed go free and break every yoke. The evilness in my heart had become a band of wickedness, yanking me back and forth in my emotions. In the aftermath of my triggers, as guilt, shame, and embarrassment tried to settle in, the weight of depression would follow, leaving me feeling helpless. When we have done everything we know to do and still do not see change, we can become discouraged.

This is why fasting is so important. When we fast, we starve our flesh causing it to weaken as our spirit becomes stronger. Through fasting, I learned that whatever we feed into our souls will take the lead in our actions. As I continued to fast, I noticed a change in my ability to hold back when I felt the urge to lash out. During that season, God also began revealing the contents of my heart and the reasons behind my impulse to tear others down. He helped me confront many of my hurts and feelings of abandonment- loosing the bands of wickedness, undoing the heavy burdens. I was the oppressed being set free as He broke every yoke!

Galatians 5:19-21 talks more in detail about the manifestation of the works of the flesh.

> "Now the works of the flesh are manifest, which are these; Adultery, fornication, uncleanness, lasciviousness, Idolatry, witchcraft, hatred, variance, emulations, wrath, strife, seditions, heresies, envyings, murders, drunkenness, revellings, and such like: of the which I tell you before, as I have also told you in time past, that they which do such things shall not inherit the kingdom of God" (KJV).

These works represent the things discussed in Isaiah 58:6, but this scripture is not limited to the list in Galatians 5:19-21. Any action, thought, emotion, or behavior you have struggled with and cannot seem to let go of- anything that does not reflect God- can be traced back to the flesh, no matter what it is! It can be cursing, uncontrollable sexual urges, or nasty attitudes. Simply put, if you do something impulsively, as if an automatic switch is flipped and you cannot control it, that is an indication of the bondage described in Isaiah 56.

When you fast, you starve the works of the flesh and feed your spirit. Doing this allows the Spirit of the Lord to work in these areas, leading you to true freedom. Some areas will be immediately broken, and others will be a process, but as you continue to press, you will experience the freedom that you have been seeking!

Dear God,

Jesus came to set the captives free! Any area over which I don't have control is an indication of my captivity in that area. I am ready to be free! Give me the grace to fast, so I can starve my flesh, feed my spirit, and break free in these areas. Speak to me in this process and show me how to walk it out by Your leading. Show me how to pray, what to pray, what to read, and how to study so that freedom can manifest in my life. I give You permission to deal with the contents of my heart so that I can be free, healthy, and whole. Walk with me on this journey to wholeness.

In Jesus' Name,

Amen

Chapter 4
Condemnation: Such A Lie Of The Enemy

For I am convinced that neither death nor life, neither angels nor demons, neither the present nor the future, nor any powers, neither height nor depth, nor anything else in all creation, will be able to separate us from the love of God that is in Christ Jesus our Lord.
Romans 8:38-39 (NIV)

I LOVE Romans Chapter 8 because it contains so much meat and clarity concerning the heart of God towards us. There was a period of time during my walk with God when I struggled with condemnation. My heart was sincere before God and I desperately wanted to please Him, but I kept falling short in one way or another. When it happened, I would feel so much guilt and shame that I would hide from God. (Sidenote: Technically you cannot hide from God because He's everywhere, but in my mind at the time I was!)

I would be moving with the Lord, preaching, prophesying, just loving on Him, and then, suddenly I would yield to temptation and feel terrible- guilty, unworthy, like a failure, you name it. For a while, whenever I fell short, I would just give in and indulge even more in the temptation, feeling completely hopeless. I could feel God tugging at my heart, but I would drown it out with distractions that had nothing to do with Him, simply because I did not want to face it.

Eventually, the pain of feeling separated from God would always draw me back to Him and Him, being the wonderful God that He would welcome me back instantly with open arms. Even as we resumed our walk together, I could not shake the persistent thoughts of feeling like I was constantly failing both God and myself. Sometimes the enemy would even try to make me feel like I was using God for my own personal purpose, saying that I did not really love Him because I kept sinning.

Then I went through a season when God began to dismantle the lie of condemnation and set me free. The best part about it was that He literally delivered me in the very manner in which I had heard most of my life that God could not do or would not do it. In this section, I feel led to be fully transparent about this part of my journey, in hopes that it will help you find freedom from the enemy's deceptive and condemning accusations.

For years I dealt with sexual sins, but as God began to heal me in this area and give me revelation concerning the foundation of my beliefs, I experienced breakthroughs in the most unusual ways. I remember being in a relationship that I knew was not good for me or aligned with God's will, but because we had already been intimate, it became an enormous struggle to walk away. I felt like I was on an emotional seesaw- I loved God, but I cared for this guy deeply. I was trying to serve two masters, and it just was not working.

It got to a point where, for me to be physically intimate with him, I had to intentionally shift my thoughts to prepare my emotions to meet his expectations for intimacy. I did not want to sin against God, but I didn't want to lose him (crazy, right?!). I felt like I was stuck between a rock and a hard place. Initially, during the times we were intimate, I could block out the Lord's voice. But eventually, I would sense His conviction while I was in the act. It was incredibly hard to stop because part of me wanted to, while the other part did not.

I did everything I could to "make it right" in God's eyes, hoping He would approve our relationship and allow it to work. We went to church together and listened to gospel music. I would minister to him, and sometimes we would pray together. I even gave him books about the Word, but things still did not come together. I would get so angry with God because I felt that if this relationship was so wrong, why wouldn't He just help me end it? There were times when we had gone months without talking, and then suddenly, he would reappear, and I'd find myself back in the same cycle again. It was so frustrating.

I began to pray that God would help me, then it switched to "If you don't help me, I won't be able to stop." Finally, I would confess, "God, I like it, and if You don't intervene, I'm going to do it!" I can remember feeling so convicted after a time of intimacy that I would literally cry because I knew I grieved the Holy Spirit. Part of me was hoping that God would say, "It's okay, I understand. Let Me take care of it." But it never happened. Amid my struggle of going back and forth, I kept seeking God—fasting, praying, and asking Him for a solution to this problem.

He led me to read Romans 8:38-39 and gave me a strategy. He said, "Resist the devil and he has to flee. But if you fall into temptation, run to Me! Nothing can separate you from My love." This may be one of the most unorthodox ways of applying the strategy, but that is how I understood it so that is what I did. No matter what happened or what I did, I made a firm decision to never run from the presence of the Lord. In my heart, even after engaging in intimate relations with him, I would immediately get up, pray, worship, and sit in His presence. He would be asleep, and I would be studying Romans 8.

The more I did this, he began to see a difference in me, and it made him uncomfortable. I did not stop trying to sin, I just kept running into the presence of the Lord. After a while, I began to desire God more than I desired him. He felt so uncomfortable that he limited his conversations with me, and we eventually drifted apart. When he tried to come back into my life, my pursuit of God and His heart was so strong that I did not even entertain the idea of letting him back in. God's love triumphed over the condemnation, double-mindedness, and everything else the enemy tried to throw into the mix to keep me from receiving His love because I had sinned.

I shifted my focus from trying to avoid sin to becoming more aware of God's love. In doing so, I was freed from a life of condemnation because when we repent, we are immediately restored to right standing with God. More often than not, we have a flawed understanding of who God is because it's shaped by man's opinion of what God should or shouldn't accept. We should not sin! We should not willingly go against the will of the Father! But when you find yourself in a place where your spirit and flesh are battling for your freedom, lean into God, and let His love sing louder than the enemy's lies of condemnation!

Dear God,

Thank you for your unconditional love. Thank you for being the one that we can run to, naked and unashamed. Jeremiah 15:19 (NIV) says, "Therefore this is what the LORD says: "If you repent, I will restore you that you may serve me;…" We are grateful that, no matter where we are in life, we can always come in repentance and find ourselves in You, and You will not turn us away. Help us to understand that, because of the work of the Cross, we do not have to work our way back into Your good grace. The penalty and power of sin have been fully paid by the blood of Jesus, and there is no price left for us to bear. Now, in the name of Jesus, I break the power of condemnation off the life of the one reading this book and release them into the spirit of adoption by which we cry out, 'Abba Father! Teach us Your ways and how to walk according to Your will as sons and daughters of the Most High God, so that our lives may bring You all the glory.

In Jesus' Name,

Amen

Chapter 5
Lead Us Not into Temptation

*If any of you lacks wisdom, let him ask God, who
gives generously to all without reproach,
and it will be given him.
James 1:5 (ESV)*

Once I received freedom in different areas of my life, I began to realize the necessity of maintaining my freedom. Throughout our Christian walk, the enemy relies on three main tactics to try to pull us back into bondage. These tactics are temptation, accusation, and deception. They can be used in any combination. For example, he will accuse you of doing something wrong, and then the temptation to respond in an unseemly way is presented. When you act upon this temptation, you open the door to deception. Whether it is convincing yourself that the person deserved your response, hardening your heart against reconciliation, or feeling guilty and believing that your actions make God ashamed of you, the enemy uses these moments to pull you into bondage.

To avoid these pitfalls, it is important to recognize those places of temptation. One of the greatest lessons I have learned in my freedom walk is not to assume that being delivered means I am no longer affected by the issue. Deliverance does not equal immunity! Deliverance frees us so that we can resist the enemy, but we have to do the work to maintain our deliverance!

I have seen so many people overcome struggles in different areas, only to end up right back in the very situation from which they were delivered! Their heart is set on freeing others from what they have been freed from, and they're overflowing with zeal for the kingdom to break those chains. They return to those areas to set the captives free, but somehow, while on the battlefield, they find themselves slipping back into the same areas of bondage without even realizing how it happened.

Once you have been set free in an area, there are fundamental measures you must take to maintain that freedom. Here are four key principles to help you grow and remain truly free!

1. Read your Word daily
2. Be filled with the Holy Spirit
3. Challenge every lie of the enemy
4. Grow in community

Read and Be a Doer of the Word Daily

Romans 12:2 (KJV) says,

> "And be not conformed to this world: but be ye transformed by the renewing of your mind, that ye may prove what is that good, and acceptable, and perfect, will of God."

Conform in this scripture means to *fashion oneself according to a particular pattern or mode*. As Christians, we are called to be transformed into the image of Jesus by the renewing of our minds. Reading the Word washes our thoughts and shapes our thinking according to the truth revealed in Scripture. But it does not stop there. Scripture is filled with instructions, wisdom, proverbs, and much more to show us how live a victorious life in Christ. However, transformation occurs not just by reading the Word but by applying its truths to our daily lives.

Be Filled with the Holy Spirit

The life of a Christian is not one of weakness or defeat but of power, dominion, and authority in Christ Jesus. In Acts 1, Jesus instructed the apostles to go to the upper room and wait, promising they would receive power when the Holy Spirit came upon them.

> "But you shall receive power when the Holy Spirit has come upon you; and you shall be witnesses to Me in Jerusalem, and in all Judea and Samaria, and to the end of the earth" (1:8, NIV).

Then in Acts 2, they received the promise of the Holy Spirit and spoke in other tongues.

> "And they were all filled with the Holy Spirit and began to speak with other tongues as the Spirit gave them utterance" (2:4, ESV).

According to the Word, when we are filled with the Holy Spirit and speaking in other tongues, we have power. The Holy Spirit, a promise from Jesus to the apostles, is one of the greatest gifts we can receive as Christians. Praying in tongues has numerous benefits for a Christian. It strengthens and builds us up spiritually. On days when you feel down, praying in the Spirit can help shift your spirit. When we pray in tongues, our spirit is communicating directly with God. In other words, we are praying without hindrances or blockages,

Challenge Every Lie of the Enemy

Once you have been set free, it is vital to replace old negative thoughts with the truth of God's Word. Remember, not every thought that comes to your mind is your own thought. You take ownership of a thought when you accept it as true in your life. Any thought that does not align with what God's Word says about you, your life, your future, or His promises should be confronted and replaced with the truth of Scripture. By doing this, you replace the enemy's negative dialogue with God's truth, establishing a renewed way of thinking.

Grow within a Community of Other Christians

In today's world, living in isolation has become increasingly common, especially in the wake of the pandemic. It is not unusual to see posts on social media showcasing hacks, memes, and reels that highlight the life of an introvert. Whether you are an introvert, extrovert, or ambivert, in the Kingdom of God, we were created to be interdependent. We need one another to grow, mature, and fulfill the purpose God has called us to do. Hebrews 10:25 (NLT) reminds us,

> "And let us not neglect our meeting together, as some people do, but encourage one another, especially now that the day of his return is drawing near."

As Christians we should be going from glory to glory and faith to faith. This happens within the community of fellow believers. In this space, God uses people to challenge us, reveal areas in need of healing, refine our strengths, and so much more. Community serves as a mirror, helping us see how closely we resemble Jesus as we continue to grow in our daily walk with Him!

Dear God,

Your Word says that whom the Son sets free is free indeed! Thank You for the freedom that You have given to the person reading this book. May their lives continue to reflect the image of the Glory of God in the earth. May Your light shine so brightly in them, that all will see and know they are Your disciples. Increase their sensitivity to Your will in their lives. Let them understand that the road map to victorious living is not found in our ability to be perfect or to do everything right, but in our willingness to humble ourselves under Your mighty hand, surrender our desires to You, and follow Your ways as we become more like You.

In Jesus' name,

Amen

About the Author

Ronda S. Barnes received her BA in Business Administration from Shaw University and has masters-level training in Administrative Leadership. She is an ordained pastor and a certified holistic Life Coach and Mentor with certification in MRT (Moral Reconation Therapy). She firmly believes that God is no respecter of persons and that every promise in His Word is true if we believe it. She has over 12 years of professional and ministry experience coaching, mentoring, and training individuals to apply biblical teachings and principles to their natural lives so they can navigate life successfully according to God's will.

From a young age, her strong desire to see God's people healed, set free, and delivered let her know she was called to the ministry of deliverance beyond the traditional church setting into the professional arena. Her unique mandate is to be a repairer of the breach, focusing on rebuilding ruined cities and bringing order to chaos. She teaches that the solution is following God's plan to restore broken people, broken systems, and broken organizations.

In 2020, she founded Pure Gold LLC to continue the work of helping people grow in the full stature of God's idea of becoming whole, leading in authority, and dominating their sphere of influence. Through Pure Gold, an extension of Ronda S. Barnes Ministries, individuals have access to resources that challenge, stretch, and establish them on the foundation of Kingdom Principles.

Ronda S. Barnes has three adult children and two grandchildren. She currently travels locally, nationally, and internationally as she teaches, trains, and demonstrates the power of God to the nations.

As the Whole Life Pastor at Legacy Center Church, under the leadership of Pastor Soboma and Dr. Faith Wokoma, she has the honor of overseeing several ministries in addition to equipping, training, and developing countless individuals in the areas of Intercession, Inner Healing, Deliverance, the Prophetic, and Evangelism.

Made in the USA
Columbia, SC
10 December 2024